# HOW TO CREATE A MARKETING PLAN

LEARN FOUR KEY STEPS TO DEVELOPING A POWERFUL MARKETING PLAN

## RON KEARN

Copyright © 2021 by Ronald Kearn, All rights reserved.

No part of this work may be used, reproduced or transmitted in whole or in part in any form or by any means, electronic or mechanical, including photocopying, scanning, recording, uploading, downloading or the use of any information storage and retrieval system, without prior written permission from the publisher.

For further information, visit us at:

www.ronkearn.com

info@ronkearn.com

# Get Your Free Gift

Email us at: info@ronkearn.com

Type FREE GIFT in the email subject and we will send it to you right away as our special thank you for buying our book.

Visit our website at www.ronkearn.com to learn more about us and please email our Customer Service department at info@ronkearn.com for any questions you may.

# Contents

Introduction .................................................................................... 7
    What is selling? ...................................................................... 12
    What exactly is marketing? ................................................... 12
    How do you define a marketing plan? .................................. 14
Analysis of the situation/Market Structure/Competition/Target Market/SWOT ................................................................................ 17
    Using Situational Analysis with Market Research ................ 17
    Internal Strengths and Weaknesses Analysis ....................... 18
    External Analysis of Opportunities and Threats ................... 19
    SWOT Profile to Create Goals and Strategies ....................... 19
    Various Perspectives for Investigating Influences ................ 20
    When to Use SWOT Analysis .................................................. 21
    How to use SWOT analysis ..................................................... 21
        Strengths ............................................................................. 22
        Weakness ............................................................................ 22
        Opportunities ..................................................................... 23
        Threat .................................................................................. 23
Objectives ...................................................................................... 25
    TYPES OF MARKETING OBJECTIVES ....................................... 27
        OBJECTIVE OF PROFITABILITY ........................................... 27
        Goals .................................................................................... 29
        Examples ............................................................................. 29
        OBJECTIVE FOR MARKET SHARE ....................................... 30
        Goals of market share objectives ..................................... 31
        Examples of objectives related to market share ............ 31

- PROMOTIONAL OBJECTIVE .................................................. 32
  - Goals ................................................................ 32
    - Examples ......................................................... 34
  - OBJECTIVE OF GROWTH ............................................ 34
    - Goals ............................................................. 35
    - Examples ......................................................... 35
- Development and Selection of Strategies ............................. 38
- Action plan .............................................................. 44
  - What Marketing Action Plan? ...................................... 44
  - A Marketing Action Plan's Components ............................ 46
    - 1. Market research .............................................. 46
    - 2. Marketing plan. ............................................... 47
    - 3. Marketing Schedule. .......................................... 48
    - 4. Measured Results ............................................. 48
  - Consider the Following When Creating a Marketing Action Plan ............................................................... 49
    - 1. Stakeholders .................................................. 50
    - 2. Timeline ....................................................... 51
    - 3. Management ................................................... 51
  - How to Create a Marketing Action Plan .......................... 52
    - 1. Analyze the state of your marketing efforts at the moment ............................................................ 52
    - 2. Make a list of the things you can do to improve your current plan ..................................................... 53
    - 3. Determine your list's order of priority. ..................... 54
    - 4. Create a marketing action plan for ten days, thirty days, and ninety days. ................................................ 54

5. Use the resources that are available to you to complete the tasks. ..... 55
Establishment of the Budget ..... 56
    Small investment ..... 56
    Big investment ..... 56
    What expenses do you meet? ..... 57
        Premises ..... 57
        Equipment used in production ..... 58
    Fittings for shops ..... 58
        Fittings for offices ..... 58
        Purchase before beginning ..... 59
        Automobile ..... 59
        Counselors ..... 59
        Marketing ..... 59
        Other costs ..... 60
    Registering setting up costs ..... 60
Monitoring Progress of the Plan ..... 61
    Why is this so important? ..... 62
    How to successfully monitor your strategy ..... 63
        Evaluate to evolve ..... 65

# INTRODUCTION

One of the most crucial features of management is planning. Its corporate or business plan runs a business. A marketing strategy is a critical component of a business's business plan. It should identify its most promising business opportunities and layout a strategy for penetrating, capturing, and maintaining positions in those markets. It is a communication tool that integrates all of the marketing mix's components into a cohesive action plan. It specifies who will do what, when, where, and how to accomplish its objectives.

A comprehensive marketing plan for a business can be composed of several smaller marketing plans for specific products or areas. These more compact plans can be prepared as the occasion dictates.

The majority of books on marketing planning are theoretical. While this approach is acceptable for business academics, it complicates the process for the average sales manager. This book takes a pragmatic approach, including the amount of theory necessary to comprehend the planning process. By working your way through this book, you will understand the principles of marketing planning. You will be able to conduct the necessary background research to create any type of marketing plan.

However, it is becoming more common for sales and marketing personnel to be tasked with quickly developing individual plans for a product or an area. This book is intended to assist those individuals and marketing personnel in developing an overall marketing strategy.

We will follow the fortunes of a company that manufactures filters and valves throughout the book – The Equipment Manufacturing Company. It will be used to illustrate and serve as the foundation for a marketing plan. All of its products will be aimed at the domestic market. To get the most out of this book, you should follow this example and create an equivalent marketing plan for your product as we work our way through the steps. By the book's conclusion, you will have developed your marketing strategy.

Adopting and adhering to the plan's formal structure (described later in this book) will assist you in logically organizing your thoughts and facts. It will be more convenient for:

- Individuals who read the plan will be able to follow your arguments and determine how you arrived at your conclusions;
- you to create a professional-looking and comprehensive document from even a small amount of data.

The Equipment Manufacturing Company is a medium-sized business with its headquarters in the south of England. The following are key facts:

Company name: The Equipment Manufacturing Company

Annual turnover: £6m

UK sales: £2m

Export sales: £4m

Operating profit: £1.05m

Number of employees: 65

Main products: Valves and filters

Provide the following information about your own company or business unit:

Company name: _____

Annual turnover: _____

UK sales: _____

Export sales: _____

Operating profit: _____

The number of _____ employees:

Main products: _____

Before we continue, it's necessary to review some fundamental definitions. Therefore, begin by responding to the following questions:

What is selling?_____
_____
_____
_____
_____

What is marketing?_____
_____
_____
_____
_____

What is marketing planning?_____
_____
_____
_____
_____

Check your answers with the definitions given below.

## What is selling?

Selling is a simple concept that involves convincing a customer to purchase a product. It introduces the concept of 'today's orders. However, this is only one facet of the marketing process.

## What exactly is marketing?

Marketing is defined in the dictionary as "the provision of goods or services to meet consumers' needs." In other words, marketing entails determining what a customer desires and matching a company's products to those desires while also generating profit for the company. Successful marketing entails having the right product available at the right time and location and ensuring that the customer knows the product. As a result, it introduces the concept of 'tomorrow's orders.

It is the process by which a business's capabilities and the requirements of its customers are combined. Businesses must be adaptable to achieve this market balance. They must be willing to modify existing products, introduce new ones, and enter new markets. They must possess the ability to read their customers and the market. This balancing act occurs in the marketing environment,' which is not under the control of individuals or businesses, constantly changing, and monitored continuously. Thus, Marketing entails the following:

- The company's capabilities
- The customer's requirements
- The marketing environment.

The marketing function can manage the company's capabilities. It can influence four critical aspects of a marketing's operation, which are frequently referred to as the marketing mix, also known as the 'four Ps.' These are four controllable variables that enable a business to develop a good policy that also satisfies its customers:

- The item sold (Product)
- The pricing strategy (Price)
- How the product is promoted (Promotion)
- Methods of distribution (Place)

The terms 'promotion' and 'place' refer to the process of attracting potential customers, while 'product' and 'price' refer to the process of meeting those customers' requirements.

## How do you define a marketing plan?

The term marketing planning refers to the processes by which marketing resources are applied to accomplish marketing objectives. While this appears to be a simple procedure, it isn't very easy. The resources and objectives of each business will vary and will also change over time. Marketing planning is used to segment markets, determine market position, forecast market size, and plan for a viable market share within each segment.

The process involves the following:

- Conducting marketing research both within and outside the company
- examining the company's strengths and weaknesses
- assuming
- predicting
- Establishing marketing goals
- developing marketing strategies
- defining programs
- establishing budgets
- evaluating the results and making necessary revisions to the objectives, strategies, or programs.

Each of these will be discussed in greater detail in subsequent chapters. The planning process will include the following:

- increase the efficiency with which the company's resources are used to identify marketing opportunities
- Encourage team spirit and a sense of corporate identity
- assist the company in achieving its corporate goals

Additionally, marketing research conducted as part of the planning process will establish a solid foundation of data for current and future projects.

Marketing planning is an iterative process, and as the plan is implemented, it will be reviewed and updated.

# ANALYSIS OF THE SITUATION/MARKET STRUCTURE/COMPETITION/TARGET MARKET/SWOT

Attempting to make the best decisions in every aspect of your business can be impossible without structured input to supplement your thought process. Situational analysis, in which market research and other observations are used to drive decision-making, can help structure and evaluate your strategic marketing plan, allowing you to make course corrections if your plan is not producing the desired results.

## Using Situational Analysis with Market Research

A situational analysis, which combines market research, identifies potential customers, evaluates projected growth, evaluates competitors, and provides a realistic assessment of your business. It entails focusing on the business's specific objectives and identifying the factors that support or obstruct those objectives. This type of analysis is frequently referred to as a SWOT (strengths, weaknesses, opportunities, and threats) analysis.

Strengths and weaknesses are determined internally, whereas opportunities and threats are determined externally. A SWOT analysis is typically presented as a list of facts, but it can also be incorporated into a matrix model.

## Internal Strengths and Weaknesses Analysis

An internal analysis is a comprehensive examination of an organization's strengths and weaknesses, typically through examining the company's culture and image, organizational structure, personnel, operational efficiency and capacity, brand awareness, and financial resources. Strengths are positive characteristics that an organization can control. They can be tangible or intangible. Weaknesses are factors that may obstruct the accomplishment of desired objectives.

## External Analysis of Opportunities and Threats

External analysis is used to quantify opportunities and threats. Both can occur as a result of external events that necessitate a change within the business. External factors could include market trends, supplier or partner changes, customer flows, increased competition, new technology, and economic ups and downs.

Opportunities manifest as alluring factors that can propel or positively influence the business in some way. External threats are those that could jeopardize the organization's objectives. These are frequently classified according to their severity and likelihood of occurrence.

## SWOT Profile to Create Goals and Strategies

A SWOT analysis is used to develop objectives, strategies, and implementation procedures.

It facilitates decision-making throughout the organization and establishes a consistent description of the organization. The four classifications are used in conjunction with one another.

For instance, a business may decide to strengthen a weak area to capitalize on an upcoming opportunity. A SWOT analysis can assist with problem-solving, future planning, product evaluation, brainstorming sessions, and workshop sessions.

## Various Perspectives for Investigating Influences

Multiple perspectives are required to conduct a thorough investigation of a business's internal and external influences. When factors are forced into categories to which they may not apply, a SWOT analysis can oversimplify a situation. Additionally, categorizing strengths, weaknesses, opportunities, and threats can be subjective. Certain factors, for instance, may qualify as both an opportunity and a threat.

An analyst considers various factors to determine the business's best growth strategy in any strategic planning process. This process examines two internal variables—strengths (S) and weaknesses (W); and two external variables—opportunities (O) and threats (T) (T). A SWOT analysis is a type of strategic market analysis.

## When to Use SWOT Analysis

A SWOT analysis is used to determine the most effective way for a business to utilize its resources and capabilities in its target market. A SWOT analysis enables a business to determine which strategies offer the best growth potential, where its strengths and market opportunities intersect, how to overcome any weaknesses, and whether to pursue a good opportunity or avoid a threat.

## How to use SWOT analysis

After identifying and listing key issues of strength, weakness, opportunity, and threat, they are compared to the company's marketing objectives to determine the best course of action. Additionally, SWOT analysis can be combined with other audit and analysis procedures to paint a complete picture of where the company's resources should be directed.

## Strengths

A business's strengths are the assets it possesses that enable it to achieve a competitive advantage. It may include brand names, reputation, exclusive access to materials, highly trained personnel, and patents, among other things. Additionally, factors such as specialized knowledge and even geographic location can be considered strengths. When conducting a SWOT analysis, businesses should be realistic about their strengths and ensure that they include all aspects of the business that add value.

## Weakness

A weakness could be the absence of a particular strength, such as a lack of patent protection, an inconvenient location, or a substandard product. A flaw may also be associated with strength. For instance, while having a large manufacturing capacity may be a strength, it may be viewed as a weakness if it is not fully utilized or is not adaptable to a fast-moving market. Other flaws may include a poor reputation, a lack of distribution channels, or a lack of expertise. Always be specific when listing weaknesses and other factors.

## Opportunities

It is where the analyst's creativity is required. Opportunities can include an unmet need or market gap, new technology, market expansion, mergers, or even regulatory rule relaxation. Any evaluation of opportunity in a SWOT analysis should be straightforward; simply identify the potential opportunity. It also applies to the other variables.

## Threat

Threats can arise as a result of market changes, the introduction of a new product by a competitor, or as a result of technological advancements that render a product obsolete. Additionally, threats may include shifting consumer preferences or fashions, new regulations or taxes, price wars, or emerging competition. When examining threats and other factors, a SWOT analysis should be conducted to compare the competition.

## OBJECTIVES

According to Dr. Philip Kotler, marketing is "the science and art of discovering, creating, and delivering value to meet the needs of a target market profitably." Marketing is concerned with identifying unsatisfied needs and desires. It defines, quantifies, and measures the identified market's size and profit potential. It identifies the segments that the company is best suited to serve and develops and promotes the appropriate products and services."

Marketing goals are objectives established by businesses to promote their products and services over a specified period. Marketing objectives are the strategies established to advance the organization's overall growth.

When it comes to a specific product, a company's marketing strategy may include raising product awareness, informing consumers about the product's features, and overcoming consumer resistance.

A marketing audit is conducted to determine a business's strengths, weaknesses, opportunities, and goals, after which the organization's objectives may be redefined.

Marketing objectives are critical because they help us determine our effectiveness and keep us focused. Objectives are only beneficial if they are grounded in reality.

Marketing objectives are short-term accomplishments that help achieve long-term goals, which are typically scheduled on a weekly or monthly basis. These objectives should assist a business in determining what it wishes to accomplish through its marketing strategy. As Tony Robbins puts it, "goals are the first step toward making the invisible visible." It is not about setting irrational marketing goals that you will never achieve. Eventually, the goals must walk the walk. Setting goals provides a clear picture of what needs to be accomplished and establishes positive outcomes. Properly planned and executed marketing objectives pave the way for financial success.

## TYPES OF MARKETING OBJECTIVES

While determining your marketing objectives, it is critical to evaluate and consider your marketing plan. There are numerous marketing objectives, but the four most common are profitability+, market share, promotional, and growth.

## OBJECTIVE OF PROFITABILITY

A profitability objective is a marketing objective that establishes the expected revenue generated by a promotional strategy. Profitability is a word that refers to a business's ability to earn a profit as a primary objective in conducting business. Financially unprofitable businesses are more likely to struggle, fail, and eventually close their doors. Profitability is a term that refers to an organization's capacity to sustain itself. There are four objectives for profitability:

## 1. Margin of net profit

A retailer's net profit margin indicates how much money the retailer makes after expenses, salaries, and taxes are paid. It is expressed as a percentage of net sales and indicates how much profit a retailer earns on each dollar of merchandise sold.

## 2. Turnover of assets

Asset turnover is a mathematical expression that expresses the annual profit that a retailer can earn on each dollar invested in business assets. It is calculated by dividing the retailer's total sales by the retailer's total assets.

## 3. Return on investment

Return on assets is calculated by dividing a retailer's net profit by the total value of his assets.

## 4. Leverage in Finance

Financial Leverage explains the company's overall capital structure's use of debt. Divide total assets by net worth to arrive at this figure.

## Goals

- A common business objective is to operate a profitable enterprise, which typically entails increasing revenue while reducing expenses.
- A profitability objective may include increasing annual sales by 15% or acquiring five new accounts each month.
- The return on assets metric indicates the percentage of profits earned by a business with its resources.

## Examples

- A cost objective could be to find a new operating facility that reduces monthly rent by $2000 or reduces monthly phone and utility bills by 10%.

- If a business has a 40% net profit margin, it earns 40 cents on every dollar of sales.
- A retailer with a 6.0 asset turnover rate earns $6 in revenue for every dollar invested in assets.
- A retailer with $20,000 in assets and $3,500 in net income would earn a 1.75 percent return on assets.
- Marcy's had $15.53 billion in debt and $4.32 billion in equity at the end of 2016, giving it a financial leverage score of 3.59.

## OBJECTIVE FOR MARKET SHARE

A market share objective specifies the share of the market that an organization wishes to capture. Market share expansion is a primary objective of the business. The primary advantage of using market share as a proxy for business performance is that it is less susceptible to macroeconomic variables such as the economy's state or tax policy changes.

## Goals of market share objectives

- Any business's ultimate goal is to increase market share. Market share expansion is an unavoidable goal of any comprehensive marketing strategy.
- Tracking a company's new customer acquisition rate allows for an accurate assessment of a marketing plan's contribution to market share growth.

## Examples of objectives related to market share

- A market share objective could be to achieve a 25% market share for product 'A' within the first three years of launch.
- Additionally, the goal could be to boost the percentage of customers who rate services as excellent from 75% to 80% within two years.

## PROMOTIONAL OBJECTIVE

A promotional objective aims to increase awareness of a company's products and services. It is the desired level of product awareness. The promotional objective is integrated into the broader strategy. The first stage of a marketing campaign is to establish a brand identity through imagery and punchlines, followed by expanded messaging via email or social media.

Promotion objectives must be defined and planned. You should decide what you want to accomplish first and then decide on the incentives you want to offer.

## Goals

**Increase business:** A business's primary objective is to attract new customers. It can be accomplished through various promotional activities, including targeted advertising campaigns, hosting special events, and launching a social media blitz. The goal is to reach out to potential new customers and offer them an incentive to do business with you.

**Increase sales:** Once an organization has established a client base, the next promotional activity is to increase their spending, which means convincing customers to purchase additional products or products that are more expensive than those that initially attracted them to the business.

**Encourage repeat business:** This objective aims to convert one-time customers into regular customers through special offers, sales notices, special perks, and two-for-one deals.

**Brand awareness:** Brand awareness is another critical objective of marketing. It can be accomplished by maintaining consistency across all marketing messages and utilizing affordable promotional products.

**New Product Introduction:** The objective of promoting a new product launch enables a business to expand its reach into new markets while retaining its existing customer base.

**Examples**
- Utilizing customer reward cards that keep track of the customer's purchases and generate coupons for comparable products.
- Collecting contact information from customers and adding one-time purchasers to a mail advertising list.
- Distribute promotional items such as fridge magnets, pens, and cups that feature your company's logo or image.
- A cleaning company may introduce home repairs to attract new customers seeking home repair services while cross-selling to existing customers who already use the company for cleaning services.

## OBJECTIVE OF GROWTH

A growth objective assesses the business's current size and formulates or plans growth strategies to achieve the desired growth level. Growth is a critical objective because it results in increased revenue. By focusing on growth, businesses can increase market share, improve sales efficiency, and raise brand awareness, resulting in increased profits.

## Goals

- The goal of any business is to expand its operations. Goals that include decision-making within a business to close the gap between current and projected earnings.
- Competitive landscape- Certain organizations strive for expansion to adapt to changes in the competitive landscape. Growth is a strategic objective that enables a business to improve its competitive position.
- Customer preferences and attitudes-Customer preferences and attitudes are subject to change regularly. A company's growth objective may be to respond to those changes.

## Examples

- Suppose you own a franchised location. The objective may be to add five additional units over five years. In this case, the objective might be to visit a new city every quarter or to reduce franchise fees by 15% for the next six months.

- Providing superior products or services than its competitors
- Maintaining or establishing a strong market position for a specific product or in a highly competitive market.
- Businesses strive to improve their services through economies of scale.

Marketing objectives are not synonymous with marketing goals. Marketing objectives can be both long- and short-term in nature. Marketing objectives should align with your business's financial objectives, which can be quantified in terms of units sold, dollars, market share, sales, return on advertising expenditures, awareness, and sales conversion rates, among others. Marketing objectives are long-term endeavors. Objectives are subsets of marketing goals. Marketing objectives should be realistic in terms of what can be accomplished, how motivated you are, and the available resources. Setting realistic, attainable goals requires motivation and capability.

# DEVELOPMENT AND SELECTION OF STRATEGIES

You can expand your business by utilizing your product knowledge to acquire new customers. You've almost certainly invested time and money developing your product or service offering. If you're satisfied with your current offering, expanding your strategy into new markets makes sense. It is what is appropriately referred to as a market development strategy. If you've identified new markets as potential opportunities, employ these strategies to penetrate them.

Consider the following points before implementing a market development strategy:

- Is the market desirable? (To truly answer this question, I recommend conducting market research to corroborate your intuition.)
- Are you prepared to put the money, time, and resources required to establish a stronghold in this new market?

- Is it possible to adapt your business to the new market?
- Are you going to be able to maintain your current competitive edge in this new market?

How can you grow if you continue to do what you're doing now? This is how:

**Increase the frequency of use of existing customers:** You accomplish this objective by

- Increasing the purchase's size
- Maximizing the rate of obsolescence of products
- Discovering new uses for your product
- Promoting other uses
- Providing incentives to encourage increased use

**Attracting customers away from competitors:** You attract customers away from competitors by differentiating yourself from them, increasing your advertising efforts, or lowering your prices.

**Attract nonusers to purchase your products:** This can be accomplished by offering your products' trial uses, adjusting the price upward or downward, and promoting other uses (check out the following Example icon for details).

**Geographic Expansion:** When considering expansion, consider the area in which you wish to cultivate new business. You have several options.: other regions, nationally, or internationally. Geographic expansion is an excellent strategy for a business seeking to expand its service territory, as it requires a physical location to serve its customers. Numerous business titans, including McDonald's, Wal-Mart, and Home Depot, have expanded their operations internationally. On a smaller scale, numerous microbreweries have expanded their geographical reach by opening new locations in various metro areas and airports throughout the United States.

<u>If you're considering expanding your product line or developing new products, consider the following:</u>

- Is the added value or new feature beneficial to your customer? Are they requesting expansions to the existing product line?
- Are there potential cost savings associated with an expanded product line in manufacturing, marketing, and distribution? Are you able to share existing costs across new products or services?
- Is it possible to use your existing assets, such as your brand, marketing, and distribution, with the new product?
- Are you equipped with the necessary skills and resources to develop and manufacture the proposed products?

After giving product development some thought and deciding to go all-in, here's how to develop new products and services that meet your market's needs:

- **By extending your existing products, you can add new features or services.** Cell phone companies, for example, sell add-on media packages that include text messaging, different ring tones, and Internet access. Several ways to expand your current offering include the following:

- Adaptation (to other ideas and developments)
- Modify (change color, motion, sound, odor, form, shape)
- Increase (more for a higher price, stronger, longer, extra value)
- Reduce (smaller, trial version, shorter, lighter)
- Switch to (other ingredients, processes, power)
- Merge (other options, products, ideas, assortments)

❖ **Create new models and sizes of your existing products.** For instance, the iPod was expanded to include the iPod mini and iPod nano.

❖ **Create completely new products.** Typically, you will leverage your brand recognition in this case. Gerber manufactures baby clothes, and a CPA firm that expanded from tax work to financial planning are two good examples of this development.

# ACTION PLAN

## What Marketing Action Plan?

A strategic marketing plan is a critical component of a business's success. Without it, the business's message and purpose will become unheard of. If taken literally, a marketing action plan is essentially nothing more than words on paper. However, if specific procedures and processes are specified and detailed task descriptions, action can be taken to complete such tasks. Keeping this in mind, a marketing action plan enables you to elaborate on the marketing strategies you intend to implement.

A marketing action plan is a record that details the marketing strategies you intend to employ to reach your target demographic with your message. It contains all of the details about the marketing strategy that the business wishes to employ, from content creation to social media engagement, SEO to SEM, inbound marketing, and online presence to traditional outbound campaigns. These features come together in the marketing action plan to create a unified message that potential customers can easily understand.

With this in mind, a marketing action plan helps emphasize the critical nature of flawlessly executing the marketing strategies established. The plan's specific and accurate information defines what should be done and how it should be done. Additionally, the plan includes all of the details that distinguish your business from competitors. It assists you in differentiating your business from those of your competitors. Additionally, because the goal is explicitly stated in the plan, it ensures that your entire team is on board.

As a result, a marketing action plan is a valuable document that enables a company's marketing team to remain focused on the marketing objective. It provides direction to the entire team on how to execute the strategies with the utmost precision. Additionally, it assists the team in comprehending the primary reason for the necessity of proper marketing strategy execution.

# A Marketing Action Plan's Components

A marketing action plan is necessary to ensure that you understand and understand even the tiniest details regarding the marketing strategies that your business should employ. It will assist you in becoming fully aware of the steps required to market and sell your business and its products or services. In that case, you must be aware of the critical contents that your marketing action plan must contain. As such, the following is a summary of the important contents:

## 1. Market research

Market research should not be a one-time event; it should be a continuous process that allows you to stay current on your target demographic's needs, desires, and lifestyles. You can gather data from your interactions with customers and other sources such as sales records, website analytics, and social media interactions.

You can also hire third-party agencies to research on your behalf so that you can stay current on trends in your target market and on media properties in which you are interested in advertising to determine who their readers, viewers, or listeners, etc., are.

## 2. Marketing plan.

A marketing plan details the marketing efforts or strategies you intend to employ to reach the first section's customers. Outdoor advertising, social media, radio advertising, online pay-per-click advertising, and public relations are just a few of the most common marketing strategies or methods used for this purpose. However, you should remember that your chosen method is the most effective and affordable based on your research. Additionally, it is critical to keep in mind that your marketing plan must encompass the coming year and the specific objectives you wish to accomplish.

## 3. Marketing Schedule.

A marketing calendar is a visual representation of your marketing strategy. It illustrates the type of marketing you'll need to do weekly and even daily. The marketing calendar is a summary of the broad activities detailed in the marketing plan. The calendar's purpose is to break down those activities into manageable tasks, each with its description and assigned team. The calendar may include advertisement placements, public relations campaigns, and social media posts, among other things. The marketing calendar will help you remain committed to executing the marketing plan without worrying about forgetting any of the activities' components.

## 4. Measured Results.

Monitoring each marketing strategy or method's effectiveness will ensure that you achieve the intended return on investment (ROI). It can be accomplished using online links, code, or print advertisements that enable you to track who mentions or uses a particular method easily. Online analytics are simple to use and interpret; they will help you determine which advertisements or mentions bring customers to your site and track which customers make a purchase. Regular evaluation of which marketing methods generate the most sales and do not ensure that your marketing is tailored to your customers' needs and desires.

## Consider the Following When Creating a Marketing Action Plan

When it comes to creating a marketing action plan, there is no standard format; it all comes down to personal preference. Regardless of the format, you must be able to present the necessary information understandably. It must include the following provisions:

- ✓ **What:** Attends to each specified objective.
- ✓ **How:** Describes the tactics, or what must be done, to accomplish each objective.

- ✓ **Who:** Identifies the individuals responsible for completing each tactic.
- ✓ **When:** Assigns a critical and detailed timeframe for completing each tactic.
- ✓ **Metrics:** Outlines the process by which each tactic will be evaluated and measured with the overall objectives and strategy.

However, putting that aside. There are still some considerations to make when creating a marketing action plan. While those factors are critical, you still require supporting data to ensure your marketing action plan's effectiveness. As a result, the following are some additional considerations:

## 1. Stakeholders.

It is critical when developing a marketing strategy to determine which stakeholders to involve to implement the strategy effectively. The stakeholder's section of your plan is directly related to the "who" section. They will essentially have a say in what needs to be done, all the more so given their involvement in marketing planning. Additionally, they comprise the implementation team's nucleus.

## 2. Timeline.

To monitor the overall plan's performance, it's critical to break the marketing plan down into short- and long-term goals. Subsequently, it will help you determine whether the plan should be altered to keep you on track. Keep in mind that your marketing action plan's timeline should correspond to the timelines for your goals. Additionally, the marketing action plan must be a living document; it should be updated regularly in conjunction with the overall plan.

## 3. Management.

Several stakeholders are required to carry out the marketing action plan. Additionally, the plan must include critical timelines for bringing the product to market. Apart from that, the plan will develop advertising materials, modify packaging, and conduct staff training. To avoid delays in timelines that could harm the rest of the plan, you should establish a regular Work In Progress (WIP) meeting. It will enable you to stay on top of issues, communicate updates, track deliverables, and, if necessary, crack the whip to keep things moving.

## How to Create a Marketing Action Plan

Now that you have a clear understanding of how a marketing action plan can benefit your business, the next step is developing the plan. However, you must still learn the associated process. Bear in mind that the final plan is only as good as the process you follow precisely. Thus, here is a straightforward guide to creating a marketing action plan:

### 1. Analyze the state of your marketing efforts at the moment

The first step in creating a marketing action plan is to assess your objectives and the activities you are currently undertaking to accomplish them. It will help you determine whether you have achieved some of those goals while falling short of others. This step's primary objective is to hold both you and your team accountable for determining which methods are effective and which should be improved or replaced.

## 2. Make a list of the things you can do to improve your current plan.

While you may be completely immersed in your current work, you must be able to reflect on what you are doing and, perhaps, what you should be doing. By doing so, you can generate some significant and effective opportunities that will enable you to accomplish your objectives. This process will generate a list of actions and pursuits that you should have taken. The list will then serve as a guide for what tasks you should complete and how to accomplish them more efficiently.

## 3. Determine your list's order of priority.

Regardless of the number of items on your list, it is critical to know which ones to tackle first. Rather than attempting to accomplish everything at once, you must prioritize your list. It can be accomplished efficiently by assessing the impact of the items on your list on your business and the amount of effort, time, and resources required to execute them properly. Once that is accomplished, prioritize the projects with the greatest impact and ease of execution. Additionally, you may discover that certain items on your list are interconnected and grouped into larger projects.

## 4. Create a marketing action plan for ten days, thirty days, and ninety days.

Now that you've established your priorities, you can concentrate on the actions necessary to accomplish your objectives. Separate tasks and establish who will do what and when. As your task list grows longer, you can begin planning and organizing the actions you need to take over the next ten days, thirty days, and ninety days. Bear in mind that you must strategically plan your actions if you wish to achieve some rapid results. To do so effectively, you must begin with the simplest task possible to generate momentum without detracting too much attention from your primary areas of focus. You must ensure that you schedule sufficient time for your projects to progress.

## 5. Use the resources that are available to you to complete the tasks.

While you're working on improving your marketing action plan, you'll quickly realize that you lack the necessary skills and resources. You should not be concerned, however. Numerous businesses and agencies exist that enable you to leverage the expertise of dedicated teams of professionals. When you are unable or unwilling to invest in other businesses or agencies, there are skilled freelancers you can hire to accomplish your objective(s).

# ESTABLISHMENT OF THE BUDGET

Before startup, you must create an establishing budget to estimate necessary and appropriate costs.

The extent to which establishment costs increase is determined by the type of business you wish to start.

## Small investment

If you want to start a human resource development consulting firm, you may need only a telephone, a computer, and human resource education/skills. You probably already have the education/skills, and if you start the business from home, the only startup costs will be a computer and a phone. Thus, the start will be relatively inexpensive.

## Big investment

However, if you want to launch a business manufacturing electronic devices, your startup costs will be high. Before you can begin selling your electronic devices, you must acquire a manufacturing facility, machinery, packing facilities, skilled personnel, a stock of electronic components, and office equipment... all of which may cost millions of dollars.

## What expenses do you meet?

Some of the most frequent startup costs are given below. You delete the ones that do not apply to your new business from your business plan.

**Keep in mind that the lesser expenses, the better.** All expenses must be covered from the profits generated by your new business.

Expenses associated with establishing a budget

### Premises
- Rental
- Payment for purchase of premises or business
- Make a deposit (e.g., three months rent)
- Goodwill - compensation paid to the previous owner for his work on the premises
- Interior design and renovation

## Equipment used in production
- Machinery
- Instruments
- Other things

## Fittings for shops
- Cash register
- Counter
- Other things

## Fittings for offices
- Furniture (desk, swivel chair, shelves, etc.)
- Computer (printer, network)
- Telephone
- Fax machine
- Machine for copying
- Additionally:

## Purchase before beginning
- Semi-manufactured materials/raw materials
- Manufactured goods (stock)
- Stationery
- Other things:

## Automobile
- Deposit
- Other acquisition costs

## Counselors
- Lawyer
- Accountant
- Other

## Marketing
- Paper for writing, business cards
- Leaflets
- Advertisement
- Website

- Opening reception
- Other things

**Other costs**
- Patent/registration application
- Other things

## Registering setting up costs

All costs accrued in the established budget will be transferred to the operating budget at a later date. Significant investments will be transferred to the balance sheet of the business.

The startup budget is a snapshot of the costs you will incur before you can begin operating your business.

# MONITORING PROGRESS OF THE PLAN

Armies do not engage in combat without a strategy in place. Football teams do not take the field without first establishing a formation. Therefore, why would you want to run a business without a marketing strategy in place? With fierce competition in every sector, you must take advantage of every opportunity to succeed. In today's hyperconnected world, those who fail to take advantage of all available tools struggle to keep their heads above water. However, marketing alone is insufficient – which is where strategy comes into play.

A marketing strategy is critical for long-term success. It will enable you to define your market position and how you compare to your competitors. Having a well-structured marketing strategy can assist you in comprehending your customers. Not only that, but it can also assist you in generating revenue by ensuring that your ideas succeed in the future. However, a strategy is insufficient on its own; it must be monitored throughout the process.

## Why is this so important?

Monitoring your marketing strategy from beginning to end enables you to evaluate your strategy and all of its minor details. It can also be reassuring for you to catch something early in the process while also saving your business time and money. With 50% of businesses failing within the first five years, your marketing strategy should be the centerpiece of your business plan.

Every business will benefit from tracking their plan's progress – in fact, those who are more organized are 397 percent more likely to report success. However, it is extremely beneficial for small businesses and solopreneurs. It's easy to fall behind when you're first starting, surrounded by large competitors. Monitoring your marketing strategy ensures that you are reaching the right people, at the right time, in the right location.

You can monitor your progress and decide how to proceed with the next stage of your plan. Additionally, you can make adjustments sooner rather than later. With changing customer desires and needs, monitoring your strategy enables you to make adjustments based on current trends and patterns. With 56% of people reporting that their customer service expectations have increased in the last year, it's critical to understand their current desires and expectations. The issue is how to quantify results. After all, 47% of people consider this to be a significant obstacle.

## How to successfully monitor your strategy

A strong marketing strategy will give you a competitive edge by better understanding your intended target market. However, it begs the question of how you can even monitor it. Numbers are not just for accountants; they are a critical component of determining your strategy's effectiveness. You'll want to track unique site visitors if you want to increase website traffic. To convert leads, you must track the number and dollar value of recent conversions. Only in this manner will you have verifiable evidence that the plan is effective, as mentioned earlier.

For instance, Google Analytics provides insight into your website's metrics and visitors. It even indicates how many people are visiting a single page. This detailed data enables you to micromanage specific aspects of your strategy and determine precisely what works and, more importantly, what does not.

Personal interaction with the public is one way to ensure that your products or services are appropriate for your customers. It does not have to be in person. Twitter is a low-cost, time-saving channel that enables you to engage with your customers 24 hours a day. In the last two years, customer service interactions via Twitter have increased by 250 percent. Do you need your company to thrive in the face of competition? It's easy but extremely effective to ensure effective communication with your clients and prove that you understand them. If they react negatively to something, you'll immediately know what to change.

## Evaluate to evolve

Evaluating your progress along the path of your business is critical for maintenance and growth. It could be in terms of revenue or customer satisfaction. Your policies and plans should incorporate an in-depth, well-considered analysis of each stage of the process.

What is critical at this stage is adaptability. Allow your ego to be a hindrance – if something isn't working, change it. When it comes to your business and strategy, there is an element of pride involved, but your company's only way to grow is if you take the necessary steps to correct it. You have an abundance of useful information at your fingertips – make the most of it.

Monitoring your marketing strategy enables you to maximize your business plan's effectiveness. It enables you to avoid ineffective efforts, eliminate unproductive focus areas, and increase sales. However, it provides you with a thorough understanding of your consumer's wants and needs.

## What Did You Think of How to Create a Marketing Plan?

I would like to start by thanking each of you for having read this book, and I hope you have benefited from it. I would love to hear from you. Please, take time to post an Amazon review, support and feedback from real readers help every author improve their craft!

www.ingramcontent.com/pod-product-compliance
Lightning Source LLC
Chambersburg PA
CBHW050259220526
45465CB00002B/745